12 WOMEN IN THE ARTS

by Brianna L. DeVore

12 STORY LIBRARY
MORE TO EXPLORE

www.12StoryLibrary.com

12-Story Library is an imprint of Bookstaves.

Photographs ©: Everett Collection Historical/Alamy, cover, 1; Knight Foundation/CC2.0, 4; Chamath Perera/CC2.0, 5; AfroMarxist/YouTube, 6; PD, 7; Friedman-Abeles/PD, 7; PD, 7; Star Black/CC2.0, 8; Jennifer Mei/CC2.0, 9; PD, 9; Barnard College/CC3.0, 10; INTERMEDIAE Matadero Madrid/CC2.0, 11; Everett Collection/Shutterstock.com, 12; Eric Koch/Anefo/CC1.0, 13; Olana22/Shutterstock.com, 13; Kallidan1/CC4.0, 13; Featureflash Photo Agency/Shutterstock.com, 14; PD, 15; The Elisha Whittelsey Collection/CC1.0, 16; alh1/CC2.0, 17; Cynthia Macadams/The LIFE Images/Getty Images, 18; Lindsey Davis/CC2.0, 19; PD, 19; PD, 20; Savvapanf Photo/Shutterstock.com, 20; Mabalu/CC4.0, 21; FashionStock.com/Shutterstock.com, 21; Oregon State University/CC2.0, 22; Bumble Dee/Shutterstock.com, 23; yigruzeltil/PD, 23; Jakob Polacsek/World Economic Forum/CC2.0, 24; Governo do Estado de São Paulo/CC2.0, 25; Chicago Symphony Orchestra/YouTube, 26; Steven Pisano/CC2.0, 27; PD, 28; PD, 29

ISBN
9781632357731 (hardcover)
9781632358820 (paperback)
9781645820536 (ebook)

Library of Congress Control Number: 2019938627

Printed in the United States of America
September 2019

About the Cover
Lorraine Hansberry in 1959.

Access free, up-to-date content on this topic plus a full digital version of this book. Scan the QR code on page 31 or use your school's login at 12StoryLibrary.com.

Table of Contents

Ananya Chatterjea: Dancing to the Voices of Women of Color 4

Lorraine Hansberry: Bringing African American Life to the Stage... 6

Faith Ringgold: A Quilt for a Canvas 8

Ntozake Shange: When Other Art Forms Aren't Enough 10

Yoko Ono: Making Art for Peace 12

Anna Deavere Smith: Performing America 14

Phillis Wheatley: From Slave to Mother Poet 16

Alice Neel: Painter of the People 18

Coco Chanel: Designer for the Modern Woman 20

Maya Lin: Visionary for the Environment 22

Marin Alsop: Dedicated Conductor 24

Missy Mazzoli: Composing a New Sound 26

Out of the Shadows 28

Glossary 30

Read More 31

Index 32

About the Author 32

1 Ananya Chatterjea: Dancing to the Voices of Women of Color

Ananya Chatterjea in 2014.

Ananya Chatterjea was born in Kolkata, India, in 1964. She studied Indian classical and folk dance. What she learned in the studio was different from what she saw in the streets. Indoors, all was beauty and harmony. Outdoors, women were demonstrating against injustice. They were using political theater to protest. Chatterjea wanted to bring the art world and the real world together inside herself and in her work.

In 1989, Chatterjea went to New York City. She studied dance at Columbia University and Temple University in Philadelphia. Chatterjea became a dance professor at the University of Minnesota in 1998.

In 2004, she put out a call for women of color interested in dance. Together they formed Ananya Dance Theatre (ADT). ADT focuses on social justice. It brings together dance and activism. It uses dance to tell the stories of women around the world, their daily lives, work, and struggles. With the help of other company members, Chatterjea developed a new dance language called Yorchha. It blends a traditional Indian dance form with yoga and martial arts. It is the technique ADT uses today.

SOCIAL JUSTICE ART

Social justice art helps people think differently about social problems. It gives power to people who have been hurt by prejudice. It helps them imagine a better future. During the 1960s and 1970s, the Black Arts Movement stressed black pride. It existed alongside the politics of the Black Panther Party. This movement was created by African Americans.

16

Number of original dance works ADT created and performed from 2005–2018

- They perform one or two new works per year. Each explores a social justice topic important to women of color.
- The works performed in 2005 and 2006 were about building community. Those performed from 2014–2018 focused on work women do.
- Each dance is a call to action.

ADT dancers performing in 2014.

2

Lorraine Hansberry: Bringing African American Life to the Stage

Lorraine Hansberry was eight years old when a brick flew through a window of her home. It hit the wall just inches from her head. It came from a mob of white protestors. They were angry that a black family had moved into an all-white Chicago neighborhood. This experience influenced Hansberry's life and work.

Hansberry was born in Chicago in 1930. Her father was a businessman who fought against housing segregation laws. He won a case in the US Supreme Court that helped change the laws. He died when Hansberry was still in high school. She believed his fight against racism led to his early death.

Hansberry moved to New York City in 1950. She worked as a journalist. She loved New York's theater scene. She started writing plays. Another black writer named W.E.B. Du Bois helped her improve her writing. Hansberry's first play, *A Raisin in the Sun*, opened on Broadway in 1959. It focused on a working-class black family in Chicago. The characters were lifelike and complex. Many African Americans could relate to them. This was the first play written by an African American to be produced on Broadway. It was an instant success.

5

Number of plays Lorraine Hansberry wrote

- Only two were produced during her lifetime. The other one was *The Sign in Sidney Brustein's Window.*
- Hansberry left three plays unfinished when she died.
- *To Be Young, Gifted, and Black* was adapted into a play after her death. It is based on her unpublished writings.

Hansberry became a spokesperson for the civil rights movement. She talked with US Attorney General Robert Kennedy about the violence blacks suffered in the South. She was a gifted speaker.

Hansberry died of cancer in 1965. She was only 34 years old. More than 50 years later, *A Raisin in the Sun* is one of the most produced plays in the United States.

A scene from the 1959 performance of *A Raisin in the Sun.*

3

Faith Ringgold: A Quilt for a Canvas

Faith Ringgold is an African American writer and visual artist. She was born Faith Willi Jones in New York City's Harlem neighborhood in 1930. Her mother was a fashion designer. Ringgold's severe asthma often kept her home from school. She helped her mother sew and studied art.

Ringgold went on to study art at the City College of New York. She earned her bachelor's degree in 1955 and her master's in 1959. She was taught to paint like the European Masters. They were all white men. She studied African and African American art on her own.

In 1972, Ringgold discovered Tibetan *thangkas*. These are paintings on cloth. In 1980, she completed her first quilt painting under her mother's guidance. Quilting is a tradition in her family. Ringgold's great-great-great-grandmother made quilts for

$100

Amount Faith Ringgold was fined in 1970

- She and two others were arrested for using the American flag in their art. They had used the flag to protest censorship.
- The charges were later dropped. Altering the flag is a form of free speech.
- Ringgold often uses the flag in her work to comment on American politics.

One of Ringgold's quilts with written stories.

her white masters while she was enslaved in the South.

Today Ringgold is known for her story quilts. The center part is a painting on unstretched canvas. Some of her paintings are surrounded by written stories. Others are framed by painted fabric blocks. Her quilts tell stories about African American life and history.

QUILTING DURING SLAVERY

Some enslaved African American women expressed their creativity through quilting. They used fabric scraps or pieces of worn-out clothing. Some of the designs showed Bible stories or stories from the women's lives. These quilts were usually created out of necessity. Most enslaved people did not have enough blankets. Some sold their quilts for a little money. Very few of these quilts remain today.

4

Ntozake Shange: When Other Art Forms Aren't Enough

Ntozake Shange knew that words alone could not capture the experiences of black women in America. So she created a new art form called a "choreopoem." This is a mixture of poetry, dance, music, and theater. Her 1975 work, *for colored girls who have considered suicide/when the rainbow is enuf*, was the first choreopoem. It still captures audiences today.

Ntozake Shange in 1978.

She was born Paulette Williams in Trenton, New Jersey, in 1948. Her family was middle class. Her parents were friends with famous African Americans of the time. From them, Paulette learned about the civil rights movement. She went to one of the first racially integrated schools in the country. The racism she experienced there affected her for the rest of her life.

Paulette graduated from New York's Barnard College in 1970. She received her master's degree from the University of Southern California. Upon graduating, she decided to change her name. Ntozake is from the Zulu language of South Africa. It means "she who comes with her own things." Shange means "she who walks like a lion." The name could also describe

A monologue performed from Shange's *for colored girls* in 2017.

many of the powerful black women who come alive in her work.

Shange wrote 19 collections of poetry throughout her career. She also penned 15 plays and several novels. She died in 2018 at age 70.

THINK ABOUT IT

Do you enjoy making art? Maybe you write poetry and dance. What would happen if you combined the two? Would that express who you are as a person and an artist?

27

Ntozake Shange's age when *for colored girls* opened on Broadway

- It was the second play by an African American woman to go to Broadway.
- The choreopoem features seven women. They are named for the colors they wear.
- It continues to influence artists today, including playwright Suzan-Lori Parks.

5

Yoko Ono: Making Art for Peace

Yoko Ono in 2006.

24

Number of languages "Imagine Peace" is inscribed in on the Imagine Peace Tower in Iceland

- Yoko Ono designed the tower in memory of John Lennon.
- Each year from October 9 (Lennon's birthday) until December 8 (the anniversary of his death), a beam of light illuminates the sky.
- A wishing well with wishes from around the world sits at the base of the tower.

In 1945, a young Yoko Ono was sick in bed in Tokyo, Japan. She woke up to find the houses around her on fire. This was during World War II (1939–1945). The United States had bombed the city. Ono grew up to be an advocate for peace.

She was born in Tokyo in 1933. Her family was wealthy. She studied music composition, piano, and voice. In 1951, she became the first women to study philosophy at Gakushūin University in Tokyo. She also studied music at Sarah Lawrence College in New York.

In the 1960s, Ono was part of the avant-garde music scene in New York City. She made conceptual art. Conceptual art is about expressing ideas. Many of her pieces required audience participation. In her 1964 work *Cut Piece*, audience members cut off bits of her clothing. She wanted to express how poorly women are treated in society.

In 1966, Ono met John Lennon, a member of the Beatles. They married in 1969. Soon after, they spent two weeks in bed together to protest the Vietnam War. One week was in Amsterdam and one was in Montreal.

Ono and Lennon collaborated until his death in 1980. "Give Peace a Chance" and "Imagine" are two of the songs they wrote together.

Ono's artwork has influenced many artists. She has recorded 18 solo albums, some with her son, Sean Lennon.

The Imagine Peace Tower emits a blue beam at night.

6

Anna Deavere Smith: Performing America

Anna Deavere Smith in 2019.

Smith studied at the San Francisco American Conservatory Theater. She discovered Shakespeare. His ability to bring characters to life through language inspired her. She earned her master's degree in acting in 1977.

Anna Deavere Smith captures American life by performing the words of its people on stage, in their voices. She was born in Baltimore, Maryland, in 1950. She was close to her grandfather. He once told her that if she said a word often enough, she would become that word. A shy child, she did impressions of her teachers to make friends.

2012

Year when Anna Deavere Smith received the National Endowment for the Humanities Medal

- In 2013, she won the Dorothy and Lillian Gish Prize for achievement in the arts.
- Smith has had roles in several TV series and films.
- She is a professor at New York University Tisch School of the Arts.

DOCUMENTARY THEATER

Documentary theater uses factual documents to create plays. These might include trial transcripts, diaries, newspapers, and video footage. The plays focus on events or culturally significant moments. They shed light on the people involved and the issues they faced. Sometimes they call for social or political action. One type of documentary theater only uses words spoken by the people involved.

During the 1980s, Smith interviewed many people across the country. She recorded their voices. Then she performed their stories exactly as they were spoken. She called the project *On the Road: A Search for American Character*.

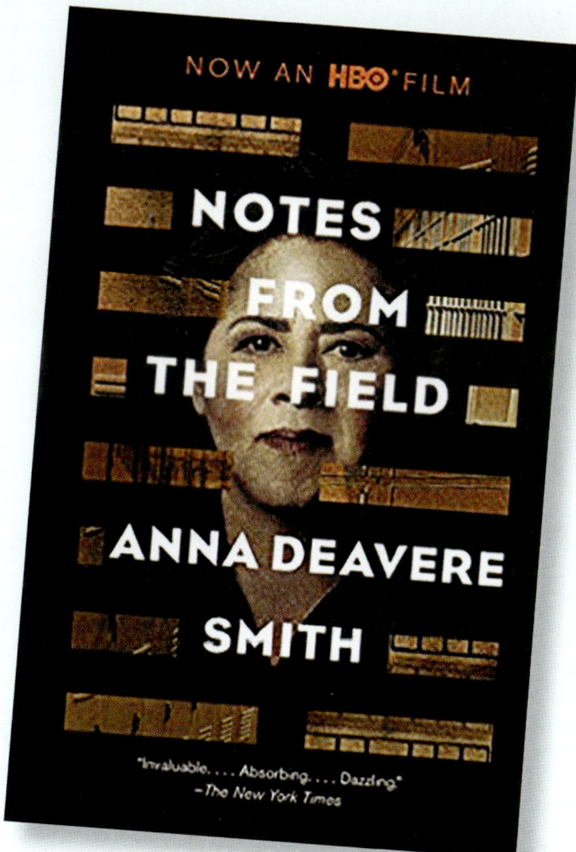

Smith's work gained national attention. She began acting in TV shows and movies. She created more documentary theater projects. One is *Twilight: Los Angeles, 1992*, about the 1992 Los Angeles riots. Another is *Let Me Down Easy*, about the US health care system. Her latest, *Notes from the Field*, is about children who end up in the criminal justice system. Smith interviewed hundreds of people for each play.

7

Phillis Wheatley: From Slave to Mother Poet

Phillis Wheatley was the first African American to publish a book of poetry. She was kidnapped from West Africa and brought in chains to Boston in 1761. She was seven or eight years old. Susanna and John Wheatley bought her.

They named her Phillis, after the slave ship she was on. Like other enslaved people, she took the last name of her owners.

Wheatly was taught to read English. She taught herself to write. She also learned Latin, geography, and history. She learned literature, politics, and religion. Her first published poem appeared in 1767. In 1770, she wrote an elegy that gained attention in both the United States and England.

Wheatley's book, *Poems on Various Subjects, Religious and Moral*, was published in England in 1773. She traveled there and met many important people. She then secured her freedom. After returning to America, she struggled to sell her work. She died in poverty in 1784.

Wheatley is commemorated with this statue in Boston, MA.

$253,000

Amount paid at a 2005 auction for a letter written by Phillis Wheatley in 1776

- The letter was written to Obour Tanner, another enslaved woman.
- It sold for twice the asking price of $120,000.
- Much of Wheatley's writing is still missing today.

THE MOTHER OF AFRICAN AMERICAN LITERATURE

Founding Father Thomas Jefferson criticized Wheatley in his book, *Notes on the State of Virginia*. He believed she was imitating white writers. Jefferson thought Africans and African Americans were not capable of intelligence. In 1829, African American writer David Walker wrote that blacks needed to prove Jefferson wrong by creating their own literary tradition. Many see Wheatley as the mother of this tradition.

8

Alice Neel: Painter of the People

Alice Neel was a painter whose specialty was portraits. She was born in 1900 in Merion Square, Pennsylvania. Neel always knew she wanted to be an artist. But her family didn't approve. She became a secretary and took art classes in secret.

Alice Neel in 1980.

Neel studied at the Philadelphia School of Design for Women. She lived briefly in Havana, Cuba, before settling in New York City's Spanish Harlem. In Havana, Neel painted poor people. She began to develop a signature style.

Back in New York, she continued to paint regular people. Her paintings showed empathy for her subjects. She tried to capture what they were like on the inside. A white woman living in one of New York's poorest, most diverse neighborhoods, Neel painted many immigrants and minorities. She also painted important people of the time, including the artist Andy Warhol. Neel talked to her subjects as she painted. She used form and bright colors to portray their emotions.

Abstract art ruled the art world in the 1950s. Neel kept painting vulnerable people, outsiders, and family

Ginny with the Yellow Hat painting, 1971.

Harold Cruse painting, circa 1950.

members. Her portraiture wasn't appreciated until the 1960s. By the time of her death in 1984, she was well known. Today she is considered one of the most important figurative painters of the twentieth century.

THINK ABOUT IT

Even though she was often poor, Neel never changed her style to fit trends. Do you think you would do the same?

$30

Amount per week Alice Neel earned in 1933 from the Works Project Administration (WPA)

- The WPA was created by the US government to help artists affected by the Great Depression (1929–1939).
- This was the most Neel would make for her work for several years.
- In 1981, she was the first American artist to have a major retrospective in Moscow.

9

Coco Chanel: Designer for the Modern Woman

Coco Chanel in 1920.

1921

Year when the perfume Chanel Number 5 was created

- Coco Chanel was the first fashion designer to launch a perfume.
- One of the most popular perfumes of all time, it includes over 80 different scents.
- It was named "Number 5" because it was the fifth sample Chanel tried.

Coco Chanel was born Gabrielle Chanel in Saumur, France, in 1883. At 12, her father left her at a Catholic orphanage. The nuns taught her to sew. At 18, she left to pursue a singing career. She renamed herself Coco after a song she often sang.

Unable to make it as a singer, Chanel opened a hat shop in 1910. Her boyfriend, Arthur "Boy" Capel, funded her second shop. She started making and selling clothes. Her designs were popular for their comfort and simplicity. She opened two couture houses in 1915 and 1918. In 1919, Capel was killed in a car accident.

Chanel had other boyfriends throughout her life. But Capel remained her one true love.

Chanel introduced the "little black dress" (LBD) in 1925. It became an international hit. By 1935, she had 4,000 employees. Some of her clients were Hollywood movie stars. In 1939, World War II forced Chanel to close all but one of her shops. She made a comeback in 1954 with her suit jacket and skirt. Her 2.55 quilted handbag followed a year later. She died in 1971.

FASHION AND THE MODERN WOMAN

In the early 1900s, women wore corsets and heavily decorated dresses. Chanel favored simple clothing. Her skirts were cut just above the ankle. She worked mostly in navy, white, beige, and black. She tailored men's jackets for women and used comfortable fabric. Chanel's designs gave women freedom from the restrictive clothing of the past.

A classic Chanel suit from 1965 (left), and Chanel fashion from the runway today. Both emphasize comfort.

10

Maya Lin: Visionary for the Environment

Maya Lin uses science and art to connect people with the environment. Her parents fled communist China in 1948. They moved to Athens, Ohio, where Lin was born in 1959. From an early age, she was encouraged to pursue her interests without fear. She loved school, animals, and walking through the woods.

Maya Lin in 2017.

In 1977, Lin went to Yale University to study architecture. She was in her senior year when she won a contest to design the Vietnam Veterans Memorial in Washington, DC. She was both praised and harassed for her abstract vision. Once completed, the memorial's emotional impact was undeniable. Lin received international recognition.

Lin's large-scale sculptures combine natural elements with science and technology. In 1995, she used aerodynamics to create *The Wave Field* at the University of Michigan. From the sky, the waves of grass look like water.

In 2006, Lin used maps, sonar, and satellite photography to create *Water Line*. The finished work is a three-dimensional, room-sized drawing of the ocean floor made from aluminum tubes.

THE VIETNAM VETERANS MEMORIAL

More than 1,400 designs were sent to the Vietnam Veterans Memorial Design Competition. Maya Lin's winning design featured two black granite walls that form a V cut into the earth. Each wall is 246 feet 9 inches (about 75 m) long. Over 58,000 names are etched into the stone. Completed in 1982, it is the most visited memorial in Washington, DC.

Lin's *Water Line* sculpture, 2006.

75+

Number of videos in Maya Lin's *What Is Missing?* memorial

- The memorial is about species and habitats destroyed by humans.
- It includes art installations and a website. On the site are posts from around the world about vanishing places, plants, and animals.
- Lin started the project in 2009. She has called it her last memorial.

11

Marin Alsop: Dedicated Conductor

Marin Alsop in 2019.

Marin Alsop was nine years old when she decided she wanted to be a conductor. Watching Leonard Bernstein lead the New York Philharmonic inspired her. She told her violin teacher. Her teacher said that girls couldn't be conductors.

Alsop was born in New York City in 1956. Her parents were professional musicians. They completed any goal they set for themselves. They were good examples for their daughter. Alsop began studying piano when she was two years old. At five, she picked up the violin. At seven, she entered Juilliard Pre-College. This is a special program for talented young musicians. Alsop studied at Yale University from 1973–1975. She then returned to Juilliard to complete her degrees in violin performance. She also began training as a conductor.

In the 1980s, Alsop played swing music and jazz. She went to the Tanglewood Music Center in 1988. The intensive summer program paired her with her hero, Leonard Bernstein. He mentored her until his death in 1990.

The Cabrillo Festival of Contemporary Music hired Alsop in 1992. She served as music director there for 25 years. She continues

4 to 5
Number of miles (6.4 to 8 km) Marin Alsop runs every day

- As a conductor, she needs to stay in shape. She stands with her arms in the air for several hours at a time.
- Alsop is known as a good leader who collaborates well with her musicians.
- She balances classical music with other genres to attract audiences of diverse tastes.

THINK ABOUT IT

Like her parents, Alsop sets goals for herself, then completes them. She believes learning to play music has helped her with this. Why do you think that is?

to perform contemporary music and support new composers.

In 2007, Alsop was named music director of the Baltimore Symphony Orchestra. This made her the first woman to lead a major American orchestra.

Alsop conducting in 2017.

Missy Mazzoli: Composing a New Sound

Composer Missy Mazzoli's music is uniquely her own and hard to define. She was born in Abington, Pennsylvania, in 1980. Both of her parents taught special education. Mazzoli began making up songs when she was five. She started piano lessons at seven.

When Mazzoli was nine, she found a cassette tape about Beethoven's life. She skipped all the talking parts to get to the music. She has loved classical music ever since. In high school, she saw a flier for music composition lessons. She didn't realize that was something she could do. She signed up.

In 2002, Mazzoli received her bachelor's degree from Boston University. Her master's degree in composition came from Yale University in 2006. She also went to the Royal Conservatory of the Hague in the Netherlands.

Mazzoli put together the all-female band Victoire in 2008. She composes the music and plays in the band. She likes to surprise her audiences with new sounds. The group combines classical music with electronic keyboards and synthesizers.

Mazzoli's first opera premiered in 2012. It was about the life of

Mazzoli's opera *Breaking the Waves* being performed in 2016.

Swiss explorer Isabelle Eberhardt (1877–1904). Her second opera is called *Breaking the Waves*. Both operas are about women trying to make their way in a difficult world. This is like Mazzoli's own life. Very few operas are written by women. In 2018, Mazzoli was named the Chicago Symphony Orchestra's composer-in-residence. She has won several awards and honors. Mazzoli is one of the most exciting young composers working today, male or female.

1.3

Percent of works written by women performed by American orchestras in 2016–2017

- Missy Mazzoli's women-led Luna Composition Lab encourages girls to compose.
- The lab is for girls aged 13–19. It includes one-on-one mentorships with experienced female composers.
- None of Mazzoli's teachers were women. She believes it is important for children to have mentors that look like them.

Out of the Shadows

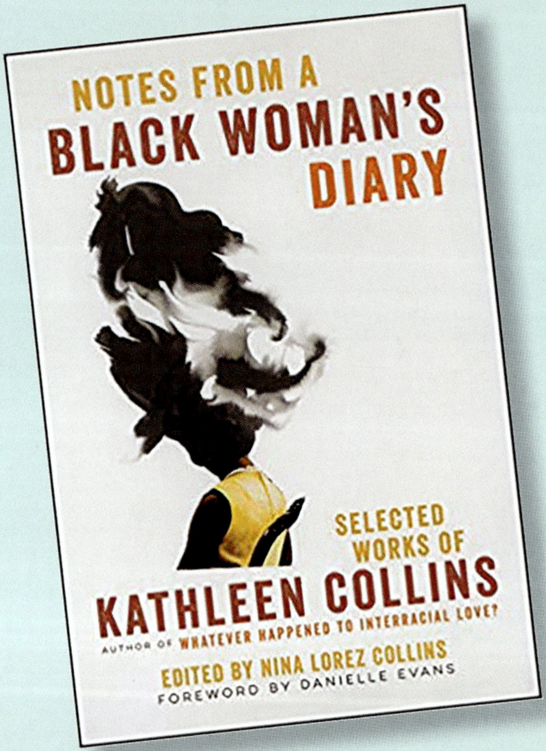

Kathleen Collins

Born in 1942, Collins was one of the first black women to direct a feature film released in the United States. She considered herself a writer first. She wrote many plays and screenplays. After her death in 1986, a collection of her short stories was discovered. It was published in 2016.

Guerrilla Girls

Founded in 1985, the Guerrilla Girls are feminist activist artists who protest gender inequality in the art world and in society. To date, the group has had more than 55 members. They wear gorilla masks and keep their real identities anonymous. They spread their message through posters, billboards, and street projects.

Clara Driscoll working in Tiffany Studios in 1901.

Clara Driscoll

Louis Comfort Tiffany was one of America's most famous artists. He was best known for his work in stained glass. Around 1888, Clara Driscoll started a job at Tiffany Studios. Officially, she was head of the Women's Glass Cutting Department and one of the "Tiffany Girls." In fact, Driscoll designed some of Tiffany's most famous lamps. In 1909, she left the company. Tiffany took credit for her work.

Fanny Mendelssohn

Mendelssohn was born in Germany in 1805. She played piano better than her brother Felix. She composed about 500 musical compositions. Felix's compositions became famous. He is known today as a great composer. Mendelssohn was close to her brother. At least six of her pieces were published under his name.

Glossary

abstract
Art that uses colors, lines, shapes, and marks to express ideas or emotions. It does not try to look like actual things or people in our everyday world.

avant-garde
A group that creates new ways of making art, literature, music, and more.

cassette tape
A length of magnetic tape in a plastic case, used for recording and playing back audios and videos.

censorship
Removing materials thought to be bad for society.

couture
Women's clothing designed especially for an individual woman. Seen as very fashionable.

elegy
A poem about someone who has died.

figurative
Art that shows people and things the way they really look. Not abstract.

memorial
Something that honors people who have died, or represents an event where many people died.

portraiture
Making a painting of a person's face.

retrospective
An exhibition of work from an artist's past.

segregation
Separating people because they belong to a certain group, such as a race.

synthesizer
An electronic device that captures and imitates sounds.

Read More

Amson-Bradshaw, Georgia. *Amazing Artists and Designers*. Brilliant Women. Hauppauge, NY: Barrons Educational Series, Inc., 2018.

Lasky, Kathryn. *A Voice of Her Own: The Story of Phillis Wheatley, Slave Poet*. Cambridge, MA: Candlewick Press, 2003.

Levine, Robert. *A Child's Introduction to the Orchestra*. Revised edition. New York: Black Dog & Leventhal, 2019.

Rubin, Susan Goldman. *Coco Chanel: Pearls, Perfume, and the Little Black Dress*. New York: Abrams Books for Young Readers, 2018.

Shange, Ntozake. *Ellington Was Not a Street*. New York: Simon & Schuster Books for Young Readers, 2004.

Index

Alsop, Marin, 24-25

Chanel, Coco, 20-21
Chatterjea, Ananya, 4-5
composers, 26-27, 29
conceptual artist, 12-13

dancer, 4-5
documentary theater, 15

fashion designer, 20-21

Hansberry, Lorraine, 6-7

Lin, Maya, 22-23

Mazzoli, Missy, 26-27
musicians, 12-13, 26-27

Neel, Alice, 18-19

orchestra conductor, 24-25
Ono, Yoko, 12-13
opera, 27

painter, 18-19
performer, 14-15
poets, 10-11, 16-17

racism, 6, 10

Ringgold, Faith, 8-9

sculptor, 22-23
Shange, Ntozake, 10-11
Smith, Anna Deavere, 14-15
social justice, 4-5

visual artist, 8-9

Wheatley, Phillis, 16-17
writers, 6-7, 8-9, 10-11, 16-17, 28

About the Author

Brianna L. DeVore has a bachelor's degree in women's studies and works in the publishing industry. She lives in Minnesota with her husband, cat, and two dogs.